Life is Making Memories

A Collection of Poetry

By Sarah Jane Lavery

ISBN:1940128242
ISBN-13:978-1940128245

Dedication

In all things in my life, I am dedicated to the Holy Family.

For years, the initials +J M J+ have graced the pages of all my communication. For over twenty years, +J M J+ has been on the license plates of my car.

I try to embrace every opportunity to thank, honor and share the blessings of the Holy Family. Therefore, this book is dedicated to Jesus, Mary and Joseph, The Holy Family.

+ J M J +

Acknowledgements

I thank God for His Holy Family, for my family and extended family who have been sources of inspiration, encouragement and assistance in the publishing of this collection.

I thank Sister Mary Rose, DMML, without whom this collection may still be a dream rather than a reality. I am so very grateful for all her assistance and encouragement.

I am grateful to Mother Paul Marie, DMML, and all the Daughters of Mary, Mother of Healing Love for their loving support, prayers and friendship.

I thank Jeanne Degen for her generosity and assistance.

God has blessed me with five wonderful daughters, Kimberly M. Kunkel, Kelly M. Dunn, Teresa M. Tarr and Meghan M. Vasil who have supported and encouraged me; as well as Mari-Beth M. Barrett (deceased), who has been the source of inspiration for much of my writing.

Special thanks to Geoffrey and Teresa M. Tarr, for their invaluable technical support and help with the photo selections.

I am grateful to my parents, David and Victoria Siembor Lavery, for my life and the many gifts I inherited from both, especially the love of God, family, and of music and literature.

I am grateful to my siblings, Kathleen Lavery Chandler (deceased), Maureen Lavery Donovan, David J. Lavery, Jr., Thomas P. Lavery, Patricia Lavery Thomas, Owen E. Lavery (deceased), Joanne Lavery Leithner and Eileen Lavery Goldych for our lives in The Lavery Family Memories. We were so blessed to grow up in a family of nine children.

I thank God for the many priests through whom God has provided me with spiritual guidance and encouragement.

Thank you to Father Michael Bassano, now a Maryknoll missionary, who guided me for many years in Utica, NY; for reading my early poetry and always encouraging me.

I thank Father Francis Pompei, OFM, Father Fred Pompei, Father Richard Dellos, and Father Gary Fukes, Utica, NY for their guidance and encouragement in using the spiritual gifts.

Thank you to Father Maurice Larochelle, who read some of my first poems for greeting cards and encouraged me.

I thank Father Marc R. Montminy, who has continued to guide and encourage me and been a source of strength for me and my family for over twenty five years.

For others who have nudged me to publish, especially my brother Tom, I offer my heartfelt gratitude. Thank you to Elizabeth Frank, Elizabeth Droz and Barbara Gaylord, Utica, NY for your prayers and encouragement over the years.

I thank the Holy Angels God sends me daily, especially my guardian angel, Eva.
.

I am deeply grateful to the Holy Spirit, without whose inspiration, I would never have written anything.

TABLE OF CONTENTS

Introduction

As one of nine children and later in life as
the mother of five delightful young women,
I often contemplate the wonder of life in the
memories that help fashion our lives.

Some memories make us smile, some make
us weep, some give us pause to contemplate,
and many we simply enjoy. Memories are often
portrayed in photos, songs, stories or verses.
Whatever the case may be, they are all a gift.

In this book, I share some of my thoughts
in a collection of my poetry. These memories reflect
my faith, family, inspiration, love and joy, among
other things. I hope you enjoy sharing my memories.
Perhaps they will cause you ponder some of your own.

The Blessed Virgin Mary

Mary Walks With Jesus
Through the Mysteries of the Rosary

I wrote the following verse while in prayer on a Sunday in June 1981.
God had encouraged me to spend the day in quiet prayer with Him, promising me a sign in the sky. At sunset, while praying with three friends, a sudden brightness shining through my living room drapes caught our attention. As I opened the drapes, we were overwhelmed as we observed the most beautiful rainbow covering the sky over East Utica, NY. Months later, I learned of the Medjugorje apparitions and the sign in the sky over Medjugorje that read MIR (PEACE). The beautiful rainbow we saw in the sky over East Utica, NY that Sunday was as encouraging a sign for me as Medjugorje has been for the world.

-- A sign of The Promise - God is faithful.

Mary Walks With Jesus
Through the Mysteries of the Rosary

In *Joy*, the journey started
In the life of Mary too
She didn't know when it began
The pain she would go through.

She was so filled with joy
When God sent Gabriel to her
Still she went to Elizabeth
To help and reassure

Our Lord was coming soon
And expectant, she knew well
A chosen few would be
The only ones that she could tell

Patiently, she waited
For Jesus' birth, remaining still
Obedient, this faithful spouse
Called to fulfill God's Will

In joyful expectation,
His total joy she felt that night
As God brought to fulfillment
The virgin birth, His Holy Light

There's no explaining her pure joy
When she first saw his face
The precious, loving warmth
Of Him sent to redeem our race

In the days that followed
In obedience to the law
They brought Jesus to the temple
Where God's chosen saw

The joy of finding Jesus
In the temple with the rest
Reminded Mary of those joys
The world would later test

She pondered on these deeply
In the joy that was the start
Before the days when *Sorrow*
Would begin to pierce her heart

She suffered as He agonized
And knew she must be still
She watched Him crowned with thorns
Bleeding, trudging up that hill.

Until he reached Calvary where
They nailed Him to a cross
Her aching heart was broken
As she endured this loss

How painful to be standing
At the feet of her own son
And watch him slowly bleed to death
And trust God's will be done

Mary Walks With Jesus
Through the Mysteries of the Rosary

But God himself prepared her
For the plan that was to be.
His gentle love gave wisdom,
Strength and guidance to be free

When each of us can learn
That Jesus died to give to us
A precious gift, His Holy Spirit
In Our Father we will trust

Then each will taste the sweetness
Of the happiness she found.
This agony was ecstasy
Just waiting to turn 'round

The *Glorious* resurrection
She trusted it would come
He ascended to the Father
For He is God's only Son

With the angels her escorts
God appointed her place
She reigns, Queen of Heaven
And Earth, Full of Grace!

The Holy Spirit came and
Filled each one just as He said
Then they believed the women
Who proclaimed, "He is not dead"

He's Risen! He is Risen!
Obedience - his choice!
He's risen over sin and death
In His Victory we rejoice!

In the fullness of her time
She, too, left the earth.
Assumed into heaven
A virgin pure from birth

Ordained by the Father
When her life was conceived
Incorruptible, her body
Into heaven was received

Mother Mary

Pray for me
And help me learn to pray

To Jesus as I seek Him
For guidance every day

You are the model that I look to
So I too may learn

To be submissive and to know
To whom I, too, must turn

Your gentleness – Dear Lady
Is the strength I ask Him for

Like you – Dear Mother
It's your Holy Son I adore

In 2002, Our Holy Father Pope John Paul II gave us "The Luminous Mysteries" ("The Mysteries of Light") and I added the following.

The Luminous Mysteries

"The Mysteries of Light

His Baptism was public
Out in the open sea
Baptized by John the Baptist
Fulfilling prophecy

The Spirit that came and rested
On Him came from God alone
God's pleasure in His Only Son
On earth was clearly shown

At a marriage celebration of
Friends in Cana, Jesus heard
A request from his own Mother
Spoken in a simple word

She simply stated to her Son
- A real need did exist
Then turned and told the servants
To be ready to assist

The miracle that He performed
Turned water into the finest wine
All present were astonished
At this miracle divine

He lived the gospel message
Everywhere He walked
In everything He did, not only
In the way He talked

With Peter, James and John
He climbed to a greater height
Where He became transfigured
And they saw His Holy Light

The pinnacle of all the graces
He bestowed on earth
In the 33 years He lived here
Since His Mother gave Him birth

Was realized before his death
When lifting up the bread
And wine for the First Eucharist
He pronounced new life instead

He prophesied in action
What was meant to take place?
He gave his body and his blood
To save the human race

St. Joseph

St. Joseph's Day

St. Joseph, today's example
Of true humility

The loving foster father
Of the holy family

He lived the role God gave him
With true integrity

Accepting all as gift from God
In his simplicity

He kept the holy family
From walking in harm's way

St. Joseph, the Protector
Of church family today

His virtues give example
For everyone to emulate

We ask his intercession
On this day we celebrate

*"When Joseph awoke, he did as
the angel commanded him…Mt. 1:24*

+ In Memory +

Mari-Beth Teresa Moore Barrett
06/09/1958 - 03/06/1985

"Think of me sometimes and think only happy thoughts,
thoughts that will make you smile, laugh
and realize how much I really care."
- Her Favorite Quote -

Mari-Beth was born in Utica, NY on June 9, 1958, the second of five daughters born to Ralph J. and Sarah Jane Lavery Moore.

She graduated from Our Lady of Lourdes Elementary School, Utica, NY and was a member of the last graduating class of Utica Catholic Academy for Girls in 1976. She graduated from St. Rose College with a Bachelor of Science Degree in Communications Disorders in 1980 and earned her Masters Degree in Speech Pathology from SUNY - Geneseo in 1982.

On July 12, 1980, she married Daniel G. Barrett of Newark, NY. They made their home in Newark, NY where Daniel began his career as an attorney with Barrett Law Firm and Mari-Beth was employed as a speech therapist in the school system. She loved her profession and children, especially those with special needs.

On May 19, 1984, Emily Mari Barrett was born. Mari-Beth was thrilled to become a mother. Three days after Emily's birth, Mari-Beth was diagnosed with an embryno-rhabdo-myosarcoma in the inner aspect of her right elbow. She was given less than a year to live with or without treatment.

Mari-Beth died March 6, 1985. She had a strong faith and love for our Lord and Our Blessed Mother. She was always joyful, had a great capacity to love and readily shared her faith.

It is a joy for me to remember her as she was and I Praise the Lord for the privilege of being her mother.

The following verses reflect my thoughts of her.

A Mother's Cry

My child is close to death
What must I do O Lord, I cried
Your Mother who stood weeping
At the cross the day you died

Was with me praying, helping me
To keep the room in peace
I knew the hour had come and
Soon the breathing too would cease

I cried, O Blessed Savior
Come and save her, let her live
But as I prayed remembered
God alone can take or give

Even though the pain was lessened
By the fact that God was there
I saw the painful suffering in
That face framed without hair

My insides felt like dying for
This child God made a part
Of me and had a special place
Deep within my heart

The anguish and the hurt could
Not be stopped but still I knew
God had not left but gently
Held my hand and walked me through

No one has ever seen God.
Yet, if we love one another
God remains in us and his love
Is made perfect in us
1 John 4:12
(Quote that appears on her gravestone)

Joy to Share

Her life like songs and photographs
And memories to share
Was one of simple beauty
Affecting many unaware

She had a simple nature
That was childlike yet mature
She loved life and enjoyed it
But in hardship could endure

Her love for all reflected in the way
She smiled and talked
And in her love for Jesus, she showed
Strength in how she walked

Her life a good example so
Each loved one won't forget
The gift of those we love
Around us living yet

She asked to be remembered
But in the way we do
God will have all the glory
And his joy will shine through you

Written November 1985
Shared with close friends and family

A Heavenly Christmas

Gathered to give praise to God
Around the throne of grace

Are myriads of angels and
Saints from every race

Each with a different song to sing
And in God's perfect time

More will join in the choir to sing
-- A symphony divine

All glory, laud and honor
Given to the King

Who came to earth so humbly
A tiny babe to bring

A love that is as gentle
As a Christmas lullaby

With power that moves mountains
And paints rainbows in the sky

One day we too will join the choir
In heaven praising now

So on this Christmas Day --
Let us be open to learn how

To praise the King of Kings who rules
The heavens and the earth

Give Him all the glory
As we celebrate His birth

Christmas 1985
My Christmas message to family and friends
on that First Christmas without Mari-Beth

Mari-Beth – A Legacy of Blessing

Through all the years that
Have gone by since 1985
I've marveled at the blessing
Of the love that's still alive

Of everything you were to us
And who you grew to be
Cherished by your loved ones
In each one's memory

This grace continues to live on
And often you seem near
We know you must be praying
For those of us still here

Mari-Beth and BFF Mary Grace Tompkins 1984

The beauty of the gift God gives
When he creates his own
Brings joy and love beyond all things
That we have ever known

I think that it must truly be
That God who knows us best
Reminds each one through every life
How much he loves the rest

March 6, 2000
15th Anniversary of her death

We Remember Her

A gift of life was given
The gift too was returned
God gave her to our family
And from her life we learned

The joy of that connection
Of loving family trust
Because of all the love we share
Remember her we must

The gift of life's expression
Is truly God's delight
When love in human beings
Is filled with holy light

It's what each one's existence
Is called to share on earth
So we too will remember -
God's plan for every birth

The way we love each other
As we journey on life's road
Is of utmost importance as well
As how we share the load

To make each moment count for God
In true humility
For least on earth is first with God
Life in eternity

Mari-Beth and Dan Barrett
July 12, 1980

Thoughts of You, Mari-Beth

Many thoughts of you today
Are floating through my mind

Thoughts that truly
make me smile
Unforgettable I find

Many days when life
 was full
And you were in your
 prime

How excited you could
be
Over something so
sublime

Memories are precious
As they bring to the fore

How life blesses us in ways
We did not see before

Times when you were happy
Like on your wedding day

Time when you were saddened
When someone went away

*Mari-Beth & Godfather,
Uncle Tom Lavery, preparing to
walk her down the aisle*

Times when you were
hopeful
And positive with cheer

Bringing joy to others
Who were filled with fear

Times when you were loving
To those who gave you grief

Many times in suffering
When you found no relief

Most of all, the times we
prayed
When we both were
consoled

Knowing that the hand of
God
 Was always there to hold

 Yes, I'm very grateful
 I celebrate your life today

 On earth and in eternity
Where we'll all meet someday.

Thirty Years or Just Days

Thirty Years ago you left
It seems like yesterday
Still I find you in my thoughts
At some point every day

I like to ponder all the good
That made you who you are
Things you had accomplished
In your young life thus far

Some people who live long lives
Never reach the place you knew
Where God shines so brightly
Through everything we do

God brought to completion
Your life in His appointed time
For us it was much too soon
But for you it was divine

Although your life in heaven
Has been longer than on earth
Thirty years exceeds the twenty six
Lived with us from your birth

Someday we'll be together
In eternity we pray
One day is as a thousand years
A thousand years is as one day

"In the Lord's eyes, one day is as a thousand years
And a thousand years is as one day" 2 Peter 3:8

Mari-Beth (age 26) and daughter,
Emily Mari (6 months old)

Emily Mari Barrett

Lavery Family Memories

I am the third child in a family of nine children.
Over the years, when writing my Christmas
greetings, I often remembered things that
happened when we were children and
wrote verses about these memories. I
then enclosed these Lavery Family Memory
verses within my Christmas card.

The first one I wrote was "The Milkman's
Helper" and everyone enjoyed it. I remembered
my brother David ("Bucky") helping our milkman,
Mr. Wheeler, as though it was yesterday.
I chuckled to myself as I wrote it. I enjoyed
the remembrance and the writing as well.
My brother was amazed that I remembered it.

After a few of these memory poems, my
brother Tom suggested I put them all in
a book and share them. I said, "Who
would read them?" He replied, "I know
I would." Now, many years later,
this collection has become a reality.

My Mother

A crowded house, children playing
Endless chores to do

So many cares and deep concerns
Joys and sorrows too

Times of darkness and great fear
Our father off to war

My mother graced with patience
Praying, waiting at the door

When asked, her words of wisdom
Spoken with a gentle voice

Would answer – God will help us all
With every single choice

Whenever times were difficult
 She had a word to say

Remember – make the best of it
And don't forget to pray!

Written for Mom on her 70th birthday
Read at her funeral

Victoria Mary Siembor Lavery
12/23/1907 - 11/29/1993

A Soldier at Rest

My father was a soldier
He fought in many wars
His heritage prepared him
To rise to a just cause

He left his home in Ireland
Marked by war and strife
As a teenage immigrant
To seek a better life

He passed through Ellis Island
Historic records show
Greeted by his sister
In a land they did not know

He joined the U.S. Army
And made it a career
Continuing his travels
To fight wars far and near

His wanderlust was nurtured
Traveling from shore to shore
From Europe to Japan, Korea
Wherever there was war

His presence in our home life
Was minimal at best
A love for books and music
Shone when he was at rest

He could dramatize a story
With such color and effect
That was more entertaining
Than any might expect

His faith we took for granted
Though it was seldom shown
He insisted from all battles
St. Michael brought him home

Addiction robbed his peace
Over the years until the last
He was at peace with God
Who brings good from the past

In the year of the Centennial
With honors he was laid to rest
With many faithful soldiers
Who gave America their best

David John Lavery
Died April 28, 1976 - Buried April 30, 1976
Arlington National Cemetery

We Were World War II Children

We were little children
On that sad December day

Pearl Harbor
was attacked
Our peace
taken away

As children,
oblivious of
The evil, greed
and tyranny

Man's inhumanity
to man
By those who disagree

Tom, David, Sarah Jane, Kathleen, Maureen
Patricia, Baby Owen

We were confused by
What we would observe

Men and women answered
Bravely the call to serve

Dad already was a soldier
Soon our uncles were sent too

To defend our country
As they felt they should do

Fear, doubt, even panic
Reared its ugly head

With a loss of hope that
Exposed a growing dread

The hush that we felt
Taught us to be enemy-
aware

Reminded by signs and
slogans
Posted everywhere

"Loose lips sink ships" or
"Uncle Sam Wants You"

"Shhh - the enemy is listening"
What should a child do?

Souvenir sofa pillows
Grandma proudly displayed

Sent from faraway places
Journeys her sons made

On every street, in many windows
Signs of loyalty

We Were World War II Children

Stars to honor heroes
Who died to keep us free

Air raids became common
Even in our
schools

Children needed to
be warned
Of all safety rules

Uncle Ted Siembor, Dad, Uncle Joe Siembor

Government Stamps issued
Bought food that was rationed

Protecting our freedoms
Our nation impassioned

Drowning out all hopes
And dreams of a new
tomorrow

Families torn apart and
Beset by death and sorrow

Uncle John Siembor

Buying stamps & war bonds
For some a sacrifice

Volunteering & praying
All aware of war's price

Women took jobs in
factories
Once done by men

To help the war effort
Till there was peace again

Stories of atrocities
Began to fill the news

Horrendous revelations
Of persecution of the Jews

As children we learned
Every oppressed generation

Knows the evil of war
Causes a suffering nation

Trusting God would hear us
We knew how to pray

We prayed for our troops
And our nation each day

World War II was over
God gave us victory

Our prayers were answered
And our nation was still free

Our First Holy Communion Day

Pictures prompt sweet memories,
Recalling each event
Special celebrations
That were truly heaven-sent

It was in 1941
The eighteenth day of May
A celebration with my sister
Our First Communion Day

Maureen was age appropriate
I was only six years old
Sister said I was "prayer-ready"
That's what I was told

Providing proper outfits
For two children at one time
In our family was a challenge
Met with help divine

Nothing blocked the blessing
My black eye or other trials
Not even missing two front teeth
Could prevent our smiles

God blessed us with the greatest gift
We would ever know
His Precious Body and His Blood
And we believe it's so!

Dad, Mom
Maureen Anne, Sarah Jane

Through The Eyes of a Ten Year Old

It was a time of fear for all
The trauma of world war
In every place on earth
Suffering near and far

I didn't understand it
But I saw fear and pain
Many grieved for loved ones
They'd never see again

In August 1944,
You may recall that year
Although it was confusing
This scenario was clear

A train filled with people
Who looked strange to me
Stopped at Fort Ontario
In our community

Watching them all get off the train
They were both young and old
The adults looked tired and somber
The children seemed more bold

They spoke in many languages
I thought sounded strange
Others who spoke English
Helped in the exchange

Sarah Jane

I heard the conversations
That took place at the fence
A fence that bothered everyone
And didn't make much sense

The Fort had always been fenced in
Since it was an army post
But these were simple families
And yet the gates were closed

When I tried to ask questions
No one really answered me
Mom simply said they're refugees
Who came here to be free

They escaped the holocaust
And were allowed to stay
In the US temporarily
And then would move away

Now all can read the story of
The "Haven"* in our town
It recounts all the details
That have been written down

But I was just a girl of ten
Who recognized the pain
And prayed that it would never
Happen in the world again

* "Haven" by Ruth Gruber

Our Home on Mitchell Street

Our home was very simple
Very small indeed

Each room filled to capacity
Still met our growing need

Joy rang from every window
Running in and out each door

Filled with God's love in motion
From the ceiling to the floor

Its facade was nothing special
A very plain and simple sight

Some shingles needed fixing
They looked more gray than white

A simple porch in front and back
With not much room to sit

Yet always room for just one more
To sit and chat a bit

The cellar very small and dark
A furnace and a bin for coal

With room to sift the ashes
Economizing was the goal

They were carried to the outside
Up the steps of cracked cement

Through slanted cellar doors whose
Wooden slats were almost bent

The red tin roof would rumble
What fearful noises it could make

When storms whipped up & fiercely
Blew the winds across the lake

But when the rain dropped gently
The pitter patter on the tin

Produced a song of rhythm
That brought peace within

The landscape was the garden
That boasted of its yield

More nourishment at harvest time
Than some reap from a field

Our Home on Mitchell Street

The berries that grew like a fence
We daily picked and ate

As well as mint and rhubarb
That formed a backyard gate

At nightfall one could witness
Observing clearly from afar

The vigil light thru our front window
Flickered like a star

Our friends would offer comments
About this sign of prayer

For all it was encouragement
That God is everywhere

The crowded quarters inside
We didn't seem to mind

Regardless of commotion
A peaceful home we'd find

On holidays and birthdays
Aunts and uncles came to meet

To share our celebrations
In our home on Mitchell Street

Sunday – A Special Day

Sunday in the Lavery
household
Was a special day

We knew there'd be no
working
But would be time for
play

Mom had strict rules &
they were kept
Despite the sacrifice

Saturday was spent
preparing
So everyone looked nice

The older helped the
younger
With shampoos and
curling hair

Shoes were shined &
clothes ironed
And laid out on each chair

*Three older girls
Sarah Jane, Maureen, Kathleen*

Tom, Bucky

In winter, there was wood to
chop
Enough to last through Monday

No washing, ironing, mending
clothes
Or chopping done on Sunday

No one entertained a thought
Of ever missing Mass

But when there was a new baby
Mom would have to pass

Dad in the Army, we had no car
And it was quite a walk

To Mass, we'd march like
soldiers
And Mom would hardly talk

After Mass, we all stayed neat
"In case we went somewhere"

Dinner was always early so
We had time to spare

Sunday – A Special Day

To read the "funnies", take a walk
 or visit family

On occasion, we'd take photos
To preserve each memory

By afternoon, the house was stilled
And Mom took time to stop

Owen   "Butch"

The black stove polished, shining
With incense burning on the top

Sometimes we went to Grandpa's house
That we called "Up the Hill"

With nine kids in a taxi
Mom made sure that we were still

In the evening, we might huddle
Around the radio

To hear a favorite program
Perhaps, "The Shadow knows"

In our busy home Mom managed
And we were truly blessed

She knew Sunday was special
And in God we should rest

Three younger girls
Eileen, Joanne, Patricia

Our Christmas Visitor

Christmas day was so exciting
Always filled with fun

The house smelled of fresh babka
Enough to share with everyone

Our family was quite crowded
In this little house and yet

There was always room for visitors
Some we will not forget

Brought to our home to share with us
The break of Christmas day

A dear old gentleman of means
A millionaire - they say

He sat amidst the turmoil of
Nine children filled with joy

And watched their happy faces
Delighted with each toy

The joy was real, with children
Gathered round the Christmas tree

No price tag for this moment
God's love was plain to see

In the riches of our poorness –
For him – the crowning touch

Was hearing from the smallest voice?
"Santa brought too much!"

Eileen - the youngest Lavery -

Joy to the World

At Christmas time, our home was like
A happy music fest

We sang the Christmas carols
That we thought were the best

The little ones loved "Jingle Bells"
We all loved "Silent Night"

And caroling together
Was everyone's delight

No one needed coaxing
To share a favorite tune

The sound of Christmas carols
Echoed from room to room

Singing often speeded up
The dishwashing brigade

As well as help the chores get done
Or decorations made

On Christmas Eve, Mom would sing
Polish carols by the tree

And when she rocked the baby
We could hear her sing softly

Sometimes the words were changed
By younger members as they sang

But the sentiment was strong
Throughout the house the music rang

One little voice we all remember
Often heard above the noise

Was our youngest sister singing?
"Joy to the World - with lots of toys

Aunt Monia, Joanne, Mom
and our youngest sister, Eileen

A Happy Quarantine

Winters on Lake Ontario
Are blustery and cold

As children, we were happy
To greet the tons of snow

But often huddled indoors
And were happy to be warm

Despite the tin roof's rumble
We heard during every storm

It was in this cold setting
Kathleen was sick in bed

Told she had scarlet fever
In those days a real dread

We also learned our family
Was expecting a new life

Sarah Jane, Maureen, Kathleen
Patricia, Bucky, Tom

Our Dad, a soldier far away
Our Mom, an Army wife

Mom always dealt with
Everything without a lot of fuss

But we knew this was serious
It affected all of us

A Happy Quarantine

The Health Department posted
A red sign on our front door

"Quarantined" – that even meant
No shopping at the grocery store

Aunts and uncles brought us groceries
And we were not allowed in school

Milk was delivered in waxed cartons
No returned glass bottles was the rule

Instead of being stressed or troubled
We enjoyed each other

There was no lack of playmates
We just played with one another

In our small home, all were exposed
We were so unaware

We didn't stay away from her
But God kept us in His care

No one else fell ill that winter
Kathleen's recovery was complete

Like many childhood memories
This too is bittersweet

Kathleen C. Lavery Chandler
03/31/1932- 6/23/1990

Happy Birthday, Maureen Anne

God formed you and created you
And named you Maureen Anne

He made you in his image
Calling you into his plan

Born on a summer's day
The fourteenth of July

A happy time for everyone
As they heard your first cry

Maureen Anne

A tiny girl with hazel eyes
And a head of curly hair

God held you close through
whooping cough
And kept you in his care

A Daddy's girl you always were
Right from the very start

And when he called you "Reenie"
It came right from the heart

First Communion was a treasure
We were allowed to share

Blessed by parents & grandparents,
And aunts and uncles there

Times of fun and dances –
You were crowned "Snow Queen"

No less important were the
times
You were called "jelly bean"

Your wedding – a great milestone –
First one married and out the door

Prepared Mom for the weddings
And celebrations still in store

Close to Mom for all the years
That she lived on this earth

Blessed with a loving husband
And all the children brought to birth

God smiles on this special birthday
For he called you to proclaim

All the virtues of the women
Reflected in your name

The Milkman's Helper

Saturdays were different
Unlike any other day

For on this day, the small boy
Met the milkman on his way

As he approached the corner
He could see the milkman smile

And motion to hop on the wagon
And lend his help awhile

The horse's hoofs clapped loudly
On the pavement as they moved

As quickly they delivered milk
Throughout each neighborhood

The ice dripped from the wagon
As it slowly melted down

And "Old Gray" sometimes left her trail
That caused the milkman's frown

Stopping at the diner was
The usual lunch treat

For this small boy, a banquet
Could not have been as sweet

Then onward to complete the route
A job that seemed like fun

Until they reached the corner where
The small boy's part was done

As they slowly turned the corner
The small boy would quickly hop

Down off the wagon just before
The horse stepped up his trot

The small boy then would turn and wave
While they were still in view

And always catch the coin he tossed
With a smile that said thank you

David J. Lavery Jr.
(Bucky)

Happy Birthday, Brother Tom

How blessed and joyful was
The day that you were born

Imagine the excitement
On that New Years morn

The family numbered five now
For our Dad and Mother

With three girls and now
A playmate for our brother

As little boys together
You played and fought and grew

Always watching out to see
What the other one would do

Playing ball or fishing,
Swimming in the lake or try to rig

Something out of nothing
You even built a "gig"

You were pretty quiet
And seemed to always keep

Your thoughts to yourself
But still waters run deep

We thought you might like farming
You seemed to love the land

With a good sense of humor
You would always lend a hand

Living on the lakeshore
Was not the greatest place

To grow and prosper but
There truly was a saving grace

The lessons of survival
And appreciation for

A life in the future that
Would afford you more

Happy Birthday, Brother Tom

A faithful son and brother
Always shared the best you had

With great love for family
And respect for Mom and Dad

Serving our country
A brave but helpful step to take

In building a career that
God would help you make

Your study, work and perseverance
Surely bore good fruit

Truly blessed
The grace of God is at the root

Your wonderful children are blessed
To have a Dad like you

May God bless your birthday
And know I love you too

Tom, his friend and their "gig"

The Boys' Dog

We had a dog named Towser
Mom said he belonged to "the boys"

He was a perfect hunting dog
And seldom made much noise

Except one night he howled and howled
The sound disturbed Mom so

During that night our Grandma died
How could that hound dog know?

His bed was in our cellar
He seemed contented there

During the daytime hours
He wandered everywhere

One day Towser went missing
"The boys" were very sad

They couldn't find him anywhere
We all felt very bad

But Mom said, "He's a hunting dog
I doubt that he is dead

Perhaps he found a hunter
And went with him instead"

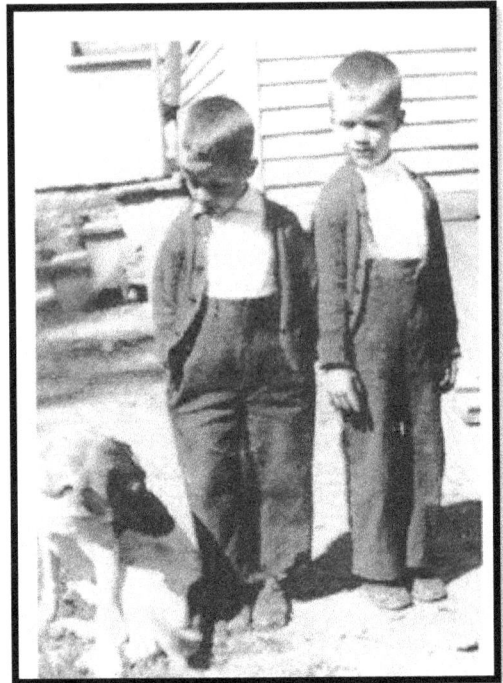

"Towser", Tom and David

A "Wounded" Lesson

It was a sunny afternoon
A perfect day to play
But Mom had other plans for me
I knew I should obey

To baby-sit the baby
Who was sleeping peacefully
In the carriage, so I thought I'd play
What harm could that be?

I took the challenge of my friend
To brace myself and swing
Across the cellar stairway
Back and forth like bells that ring

When suddenly I lost my grip
My hands slipped out of place
I fell down through the opening
And fell right on my face

A painful injury was caused
When I hit that cement
Mom said – we need the doctor
Only she knew what that meant

We were an Army family
So we received health care
Right at Fort Ontario
My Dad was stationed there

Sarah Jane
"being military"

We walked into the hospital
But had to wait until
The soldiers finished marching
A long time to sit still

We watched them take the flag down
And heard the cannon blast
The bugler sounded taps and then
They all marched back at last

The captain was the doctor
Who stitched the wound I had
Said my eye would be alright
The wound was not too bad

They gave my Mom some water
Too upset to stay with me
They put a big patch on my eye
And I could barely see

The doctor, as he said goodbye
Put a coin in my hand
Mom said we could spend it
When we reached the custard stand

My eyesight was intact and
The three stitches soon were healed
From this "wounded" lesson
To me wisdom was revealed

"Do one thing and do it well
And mind your P's and Q's
Watch out for those distractions
And foolish challenges refuse!"

Mom's Special Birthday

Two days before Christmas
On our Mom's birthday

We made our decorations
In our own special way

With red and green crepe paper
Twisted and strung

Making places for red tissue paper
Bells to be hung

Chains of red and green paper
Loops fastened with paste

Since our resources were limited
There was never any waste

The biggest excitement
Was trimming the tree

Freshly cut by our uncles
One as tall as could be

Smells of cake and fresh babka
Wafting through the air

For nine Lavery noses
Signaled a scrumptious fare

For Mom's special birthday
She baked her favorite cake

One that in the years to come
We would learn to make

Our Advent was over
Christmas excitement had begun

God had already blessed us
Each and everyone

"Butch" - Our Loving Brother

The Lavery children numbered six
When he arrived upon the scene

Four girls and two boys
Welcomed little Owen Eugene

We were all excited that we had
A brand new baby brother

But it was baby number seven
For our dear loving Mother

Times were still difficult
World War II had its effect

Upon our very livelihood
As you may expect

As a boy, his raising pigeons
Puzzled most of us

Except for Eileen, his best buddy
Who helped without a fuss

As a man, he served his country
And with honor did his best

Fathered a growing family
Not without trials all will attest

He loved the earth and had a gift
To plant to make things grow

His talents he developed
In ways in time would show

He was a storyteller
Who always had a smile

Willing to take the time
To sit and chat awhile

He had a winning way
That was like no other

For us, - the Lavery siblings
He's "Butch", our loving brother

Owen Eugene "Butch" Lavery
01/21/1942 – 12/16/2014

Miriam

For as long as I can remember
She was always there

As a tiny slip of a girl
And as a young lady fair

Early years on our front porch
Where she patiently sat

Waiting for her playmate
From wherever he was at

This started a true friendship
No one knew would grow

And envelop our whole family
Sharing joys and sorrows we'd know

A sweet and loving girl
With talent and a gentle way

Who loved one boy and knew
They'd be together one day

Both athletes and good swimmers
They had a lot of fun

He played ball and she cheered
At every game they won

They both loved music
And sang in harmony

Mimi and Bucky

A match made in heaven
Pledging their love eternally

A loving wife and mother of
A family still growing in size

She treated everyone with
gentleness
As she did her butterflies

Sweet memories we have of
Dear Miriam who was known

As Mimi, Mom, NaNa , sister, friend
We all loved her as our own

She lived a happy fruitful life
For her there could be no other

The life she always
wanted
Long happy years
with our brother

Miriam (Mimi) Galloway Lavery
8/02/1936 – 05/08/2013

A Special Place

There's a special place in heaven
Your child rejoices with the rest

Of those who've gone before us
Heaven knows that it's the best

But in the hearts touched by this child
The loved ones who survive

There is a special place
Your child will always be alive

The grace of the Lord Jesus be with all.
Rev. 22:21

"Davey"
Son of Bucky and Mimi Lavery

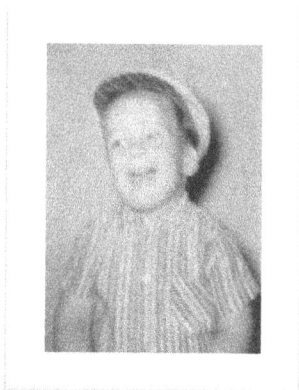

David John Lavery III
08/23/1955 - 06/21/1958

Born into Eternity

Every person has a birthday
We celebrate on earth

The day our bodies come to life
The day of each one's birth

We also celebrate the day
In prayerful memory

When each one shall be gifted
To be born in eternity

Like a drop of sea water, like a grain of sand,
so are these few years among the days of eternity.
Sirach 18:8

"Chip"
Son of Butch and Ava Lavery

Warren Hale Lavery
06/26/1982 - 02/08/1983

Christmas Verses

I love Christmas.
It seems to bring out the best in people.
I have always loved to send and receive
Christmas greeting cards. However, there
were times when I couldn't find just the
right card to send. So I decided to write my
own verses and make my own cards. They
are the product of my meditation and prayer
each year as I consider the greatest gift God
has ever given us, His Only Son,
Our Lord and Savior Jesus Christ.

These are some of those verses.

Sing a New Song

Sing a new song of God's love
Let his joy fill the air

Let the world around us know
That God is everywhere

Christmas is a time to share
The love of Christ the King

May Jesus fill each heart with joy
To praise the Lord and sing

Sing to the Lord a new song,
his praise from the ends of the earth...
Isaiah 42:10

A Savior is Born

A child is born - a baby boy
A mother and father filled with joy

A humble manger, bleak and cold
A scene to ponder for young and old

A holy treasure in her heart
A miracle within to start

A journey filled with joy and pain
A Savior born to rule and reign

Mary treasured all these things
and reflected on them in her heart.
Luke 2:19

Signs of Christmas

Christmas carols, manger scenes
Gingerbread and candy canes

Holly wreaths and silver bells
Lights that brighten window panes

Trees for trimming, ornaments
Angels, stars and mistletoe

Signs of Christmas celebrations
Everywhere we go

May these signs serve to remind us
That we are all called to be

Signs for all the world around us
Of God's love for you and me

"And this will be a sign for you;
you will find an infant wrapped
in swaddling clothes and lying in a manger."
Luke 2:12

Simply Grace

We come to God
Just as we are

As those who
Simply saw the star

We reach out
Simply to be kind

And pray
Humanity will find

Grace in a humble manger
With a simple family

Reminding us to treasure
Holy simplicity

Throughout all the ages
God's message to the human race

A simple reminder
All is accomplished by God's grace

Holy Night

In the hustle bustle of our lives
Be still and hear
In the violence and strife we witness
God says - have no fear
In the places in the world where war prevails
God's angels still proclaim
In the hearts of all believers, no matter where you are
Each will praise his holy name
In the stillness of a holy night, Jesus Christ was born on earth
The world was still, the star shone bright
In this holy silence, may we, like lowly shepherds, bow at Our Savior's birth
And hear angelic voices praising God this Holy Night

And suddenly there was a multitude of the heavenly host
with the angel, praising God and saying:
"Glory to God in the highest and on earth
peace to those on whom his favor rests."
Luke 2:13

Remembering Christmas

Happy are the memories
Cherished and retold
As the Christmas story is
Shared by young and old

Blessings and excitement
Of Christmases now past
Filled with thoughts and gestures
And joy that's meant to last

Precious gifts from loved ones,
Friends and family
Special ornaments long treasured
All hung on the Christmas tree

The infant Jesus in a manger
The long-awaited promised one
Born to a lowly virgin that
The Father's will be done

As each one retells the story
It resounds through all the earth
The story of the greatest gift
The Messiah's holy birth.

For today in the city of David,
a Savior has been born for you
who is Messiah and Lord.
Luke 2:11

His Light

His light shines ever brighter
In our world today

As many holy men and women
Lift their hearts to pray

Times of hardship and distress
Reveal to everyone

That in the light of charity
Battles are still won

As one helps another
The flame of caring burns

The light of Christ burns brighter
As each Christian learns

Let us share the light of Jesus
In the love and joy we bring

As we celebrate the birthday
Of Jesus Christ, The King!

...the light shines in the darkness;
and the darkness has not overcome it.
John 1:5

The Christmas Spirit

Holly wreaths and jolly greetings
Trees with ornaments and lights

Flying angels, snow-topped steeples
Silver bells, candied delights

Young and old dressed for a party
Carolers sing door to door

Scenes inspired by thoughtful artists
Fun and games and gifts galore

There would be no Christmas spirit
Without Jesus' holy birth

No cause to deck the halls with holly
Or angels singing peace on earth

God poured out His Holy Spirit
Upon Mary, his pure choice

To bear Jesus to the world
Who gives the Spirit to rejoice!

The angel said to her, "The Holy Spirit will
come upon you, and the power of the Most High
will overshadow you. therefore, the child to be
born will be called holy, the Son of God."
Luke 1:35

Christmas Treasures

Precious gifts were given Him
Frankincense, myrrh and gold

By wise men who were seeking
The Christ child we are told

They were willing givers
Who traveled long and far

With faith and trust they sought Him
By following a star

As we prepare our treasures
To give on Christmas day

Let us be willing givers and
Take the time to pray

That mankind will seek Jesus
Who is merciful and kind

As the wise men found the manger
The Messiah each will find!

...they opened their treasures and offered
Him gifts of gold, frankincense and myrrh.
Mt 2:11

Her Precious Son

He was born of Mary
In this holy birth
To save mankind, God sent
His only Son unto the earth

As we, his earthly family
Join to celebrate as one
Together with our Mother
Let us praise Her Precious Son

This world is gifted to us and
God tell us to rejoice
We have the gift of life and
Free will to make each choice

Like Mary, let us choose God's will
And say – let it be done
As she was open to receive
She gave Her Precious Son

He is the true Messiah,
The Redeemer, Mighty King
Emmanuel, the Lamb of God
The Healer, the Dayspring

He is the Prince of Peace, Light of
The World, the Promised One
He's Jesus Christ, the Son of God
He is Her Precious Son!

You shall conceive and bear a son
and give him the name Jesus. Luke 1:31

He is Here

Above the clamor & the noise
Of traffic in the streets

Computers, email, Ipads
Voice mail and constant tweets

Despite anxiety, depression
Sickness, conflicts everywhere

Loneliness and hunger
Unemployment and despair

Angel voices are still singing
"Rejoice and do not fear"

Emmanuel, God with us
Reminds us - He is here!

"Behold , the virgin shall be with child
and bear a son, and they shall name
Him Emmanuel, which means
"God is with us"
Mt. 1:23

Good News

Jesus came to earth
Over two thousand years ago

To save and heal humanity
And teach each one to show

The saving love of God that heals
So everyone may find

The path that leads to love and joy
And peace for all mankind

Let's celebrate the good news –
The birth of God The Son

Jesus Christ Our Savior
He came for everyone!

The angel said to them, "Do not be afraid,
I came to proclaim to you good news
of great joy that will be for all people."
Luke 2:10

The Gift

The Magi were three wise men
Each one a king

Who followed a star
Not knowing what it may bring

The star was God's light
We still follow today

Trusting that God
Always show the way

Wise men bearing gifts
Found a babe in a cave

And in giving received
Much more than they gave

Changing their course
After finding the King

Is the gift of the Savior
This encounter will bring

…they departed for their country
by another way. Mt. 2:12

A Family Christmas

Christmas brings out
The best in every family
Reminding all far and near
What love was meant to be

No matter past divisions
At Christmas time each year
Each heart awakens to a greater
Love for those held dear

The Mother of our Savior
Has shown each one the way
By her love and example and
Has said to pray, pray, pray

St. Joseph, with great devotion
Gave love unselfishly
A sign to all the ages –
- The Holy Family –

As we share love this Christmas
May we join one and all
As signs that we're his family
Let each answer the call

To love God as He loves us
And live the great command
With Jesus Christ the Savior
Of each family in the land!

a sign to you; in a manger you will find an infant... Luke 2:12

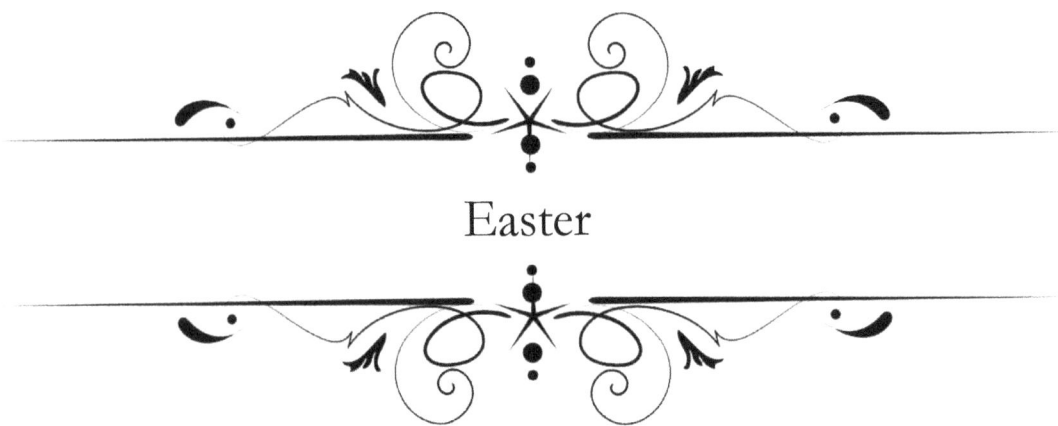

Easter

Easter is the most beautiful and important feast we celebrate. Growing up in a large family seemed to generate great excitement as we looked forward to Easter. Mom was very serious about the practices of preparing for Easter. During Lent, we were encouraged to attend daily Mass and stop in church on our way home from school to "make" a visit and even say the stations while we were there. In those days, the churches were not locked.

Holy Week was very important. On Holy Thursday, we were encouraged to walk to visit all seven of the Catholic churches (or as many as possible) in our city to adore the Lord. In each church, a side altar was beautifully decorated with lots of flowers and candles surrounding the monstrance that held the Blessed Sacrament. During each visit, we would spend time in prayer, adoring the Lord.

On Good Friday, Mom insisted on silence in our home; no singing or radios playing. She covered all the mirrors in the house, saying we did not need to be distracted. During the hours from 12 noon to 3pm, we were not allowed to talk and we each had chores to keep us busy. In those days, most of the stores closed their doors between the hours of 12 noon to 3 pm.

Holy Saturday was exciting in anticipation of the great feast. We were excited about finding our Easter baskets filled with candy that were hidden by the "Easter bunny". During World War II, when sugar was rationed and chocolate hard to find, it was a challenge for Mom to fill the baskets with Easter candy but she managed. At my grandparents' house, the Polish priest came and blessed the food that had been prepared in advance for the Easter celebration including our favorite, Mom's Babka.

In my early years, we attended the sunrise Mass at the Polish church and marched in the procession, wearing white dresses with ribbons and flowers in our hair. Our uncles participated in carrying the risen Lord in the procession and our aunts sang in the choir, as my Mom had done in previous years. As we grew older, we attended another church closer to our home but we enjoyed the excitement. Despite our limited resources, Mom always made sure each one had a new outfit for Easter. She insisted that Easter is a time for new life and we should all have something new.

Alleluia!!

The Miracle of Easter

Now the forty days have passed
In preparation for this day
We've prayed and fasted faithfully
Each in a special way

Time spent in meditating
The true meaning of the cross
Has brought new understanding to
The phrase "count it all loss"

The cross to those now being lost
Seems useless to embrace
It calls for all to sacrifice
Dependant on God's grace

It means that our compassion
Must be gentle and sincere
For each one has been called by God
And that is why we're here

At the cross are new beginnings
For each to learn the way
To repent and find the freedom
That we celebrate today

Jesus Christ has won the victory
He died for us, it was his choice
He's alive! The tomb is empty!
We are free! Let us rejoice!

He Is Risen! Alleluia!

An empty cross
An empty shroud

Bewildered faces
A once angry crowd

Helpless loved ones
At Calvary

Mary Magdalene and John
His Mother Mary

Darkness and suffering
Put to death

Forgiveness for all
From his dying breath

All evil defeated
The stone rolled away

The sepulcher is empty
He's risen today!

Then the angel spoke, addressing the women:
Do not be frightened. I know you are looking
for Jesus the crucified one but he is not here.
He has risen, exactly as he promised.
Mt 28:5, 6a

The Triumph of the Cross

Jesus died for our transgressions
Our diseases and our pain

To save the world from sin and death
His loss is our gain

He gave his life as ransom
The price He paid to save

No earthly force could bury him
And keep him in the grave

He rose! - Yes - He is risen!
He is alive today

Sing praise, shout Alleluia
The cross triumphant every day

Alleluia!

Just so, the Son of man did not come
to be served but to serve and give
his life as ransom for many.
* Mt 20:28*

Easter, Our Springtime

Springtime bursts forth
New light
Indescribable beauty
Voluminous joy

Treasures of earth yield
Fresh growth
Colorful buds
New blessings

Jesus took to the cross
Our sins
Our infirmities
Our despair

Easter is the springtime
Of our faith
All creation sings
Alleluia! He is Risen!
Jesus Christ, The King of Kings!

Time to Celebrate

God loves celebrations
Flowers, candy, bunnies too

With every celebration we hear
Him whisper - I love you

The angels at the tomb announced
He's risen! Have no fear!

It's time to celebrate His love
Alleluia Easter is here!

Then the angel spoke, addressing the women:
Do not be frightened. I know you are looking
for Jesus the crucified one but he is not here.
He has risen, exactly as he promised.
Mt:28:5,6a

St. Patrick's Day

St. Patrick is an important saint for our family to celebrate.
There are many stories about St. Patrick and his influence in the conversion of Ireland.

Dad was born in Belfast, Ireland and came to this country as a teenager. He had only one sister, Sarah Jane, (Aunt Sally) in the United States, who settled in New York, where she trained as a nurse in Bellevue Hospital. The rest of his family remains in Ireland. He lived with cousin Sarah McMahon in Lynn, MA for a time until he joined the US Army. While we were growing up, he was away in the army most of the time. Our contact with our Lavery roots was limited so we were a bit disconnected from the Irish influence. However, Mom was adamant that no one left the house on St. Patrick's Day without wearing a bit of green. She went to great lengths to achieve that, always reminding us of our Irish roots. She impressed on us the importance of celebrating our Irish heritage.

St. Patrick's Day is a special day of celebration in our family.

A Time to Celebrate
- A Time to Pray

Enjoy corned beef and cabbage
And some Irish soda bread

With all the Irish songs sung
Loud enough to raise the dead

May all your cares and worries
Be relinquished to God's care

Wear a bit of Irish green
On your lapel or in your hair

Say an Ave for your enemies
And one for those you love

Ask St. Patrick's intercession -
As he prays in heaven above

*..the fervent prayer of a righteous person
is powerful indeed. James 5:16*

Celebrate His Way

It's a day of celebration
A time to sing God's praise

For the saint beloved by those
He preached to in those days

His message was the Word of God
Spoken as we hear today

Proclaiming Jesus Christ is Lord
He is the only way!

*Jesus told him, "I am the way,
the truth and the life:
no one come to the Father
but through me…"
John 14:6*

St Patrick - The Missionary

Born of Roman - British parents
He may have lived in Gaul

Then enslaved by Irish pagans
For a short time we recall

Later on in life God called him
Back to Ireland

To share God's love with pagans
Their conversion was God's plan

*... go ye therefore, and make disciples
of all nations... Mt 28:19*

The Shamrock

St. Patrick used the shamrock
To teach the Holy Trinity is one

He drove the snakes away and
Shared God's love with everyone

The Irish give him honor
And celebrate this day

And thank God for our heritage
And for the Christian way

*In the Name of the Father
and of the Son
and of The Holy Spirit. Amen*

Thanksgiving

Thanksgiving is one time during the year
when it is politically correct to be thankful publicly.

As Christians, we know that the fastest route to
the throne of God is through our sincere gratitude
to God for everything, everyday.

However, it is wonderful that our country
sets aside a day to be mindful of the gift of our great
heritage and freedom that we share with
one another.

We are a truly blessed nation.

We Are Blessed

As we gather in Thanksgiving,
Let us thank the Lord in prayer

For He has blessed America
And kept us in His care

In a world filled with hostility,
Hunger, war and strife

Let us praise the Lord for freedom
And respect each life

Bless the Lord, O my soul,
and forget not all his benefits
Psalm 103:2

Bless the Lord

Bless The Lord
For all the blessings
He gives us day by day

Bless Him
For all our loving friends
Who bless us as they pray

Bless God
For His Son Jesus
And the grace of family

Bless The Lord
For this Thanksgiving
And for blessings yet to be!

We Thank You, Lord

We thank you, Lord
For the gift of life
For all that we can be

We thank you, Lord
For those we love
For our friends and family

We thank you, Lord
For harvest time
For you provide our food

We thank you, Lord
For blessing us
For you are kind and good

Give thanks to the Lord for He is good,
his kindness endures forever.
1 Chronicles 17:34

Our Great Freedom

The bells from our church towers
Ring out God's message everyday

Calling every Christian
To use the gift to pray

Praising God for our great freedom,
Let each repent on bended knee

Trusting Jesus who is mercy
To keep our nation free

..and if my people, upon whom my name
has been pronounced, humble themselves
and pray, and seek my presence
and turn from their evil ways,
I will hear them from heaven
and pardon their sins and revive their land.
2 Chronicles 7:14

Friends

Special occasions are often a time
of inspiration to write a verse.
In praying for the occasion and the person,
I am sometimes inspired to write a verse
and share it with them

The following verses are a few of those.

Karen's Yes

She's a woman on the go for God
With boundless energy
A servant open to the Lord
To serve in ministry

One wonders how she does it all
And always with a smile
Ready with her "yes" to God
To go the extra mile

A loving wife and mother
She blessed the Mom's Connection
Sharing with the other Moms
Her love and dedication

As she donated her kidney
She exemplified God's care
And if that was not enough
She gave away her hair

A true woman of Mary
An example to behold
Of willing service for us all
Whether young or old

Singing praises to the Lord
No matter what the stress
As Mary answered to the Lord
Her answer too is "yes"

Karen Vacaliuc
Women of Mary & Women's Biblical Ministry
"Farewell" as she, her husband and children
leave New Hampshire to relocate in Tennessee

Then Mary said, "Here I am, the servant of the Lord; let it be with me according to your word" Luke 1:38

Lucille, A Woman of Favor

God's love is very evident
In everything you do

As you share in community
His Spirit moves through you

The power of your witness
As a woman of The Word

Proclaimed in being who you are
A message clearly heard

A woman who is willing to
Take up the cross each day

And share with other women
Who need guidance on the way

Like Mary and Elizabeth
Like Judith, Esther, Ruth

Holy women of the Bible
Who journeyed in God's truth

A true woman of the scriptures
You have an honored place

Among our women young and old
With whom you've shared God's grace

Lucille Laflamme
Catholic Women of the Year
Women's Biblical Ministry
Sainte Marie Parish
Manchester, NH

And coming to her, He said, "Hail favored one! The Lord is with you." Luke 1:28

Our Father Marc

A man of action immersed in prayer
Makes time to bring God everywhere
He travels where God's Spirit leads
Evangelizing, meeting needs
Living out his chosen mission
To proclaim the great commission

For our Sainte Marie Parish family
He spends himself unselfishly
There is no end to his good deeds
His tireless efforts, the growing needs
Who can count the steps he takes
Masses, confessions, sick calls he makes

Marriages performed, nurtured to last
Many came home who were once outcast
Our parish bursting with love to spare
God's Spirit alive, blessings everywhere
Countless souls saved, babies baptized
One day in heaven, all will be surprised

How does he do it? – many do ask
Always ready for *"just one more task"*
He always answers with a smile
How he can go the extra mile
"Got a big health, don't worry about me"
His zealous example is plain to see

He inspires each one that we may too
Give to our Lord the best we can do
A man of vision with God's insight
Filled with His Spirit, shining God's light
We in our faith will ever stay strong
Discerning always right from wrong

Someday we'll see that his legacy
In his faithful service to God will be
He came to this family & nurtured it well
For generations to come, stories we'll tell
He who loves God with all his heart
Prayed each birth would have a good start

He's still Our Father, we're his family
Still growing fruit on this family tree
As the years come and go, we will recall
Twenty six years with us, giving his all
Helping this family to grow in good health
To know the Trinity and all its wealth

Rev. Marc R. Montminy
On the occasion of his re-assignment to St. Michael's
Parish, Exeter, NH after serving Sainte Marie Parish
for twenty six years.

The Spirit of the Lord is upon me; therefore He has
anointed me. He has sent me to bring glad tidings to
the poor, to proclaim liberty to captives, recovery of sight
to the blind and release to prisoners. To proclaim a
year of the Lord's favor. Luke 4: 18, 19

Shine On

During Morning Mass at St. Joseph's
Truly God's light shone
So brightly through a young priest
It was clear that God alone

Had ordained him special
On that day in '91
Providing for the path he'd walk
That God's will be done

Accepting God's direction
As he moved from post to post
He shared God's gifts with joyful love
Proclaiming God his boast

As servant to the bishop
To God's people became known
To be faithful to his calling
Preaching seeds of faith well sown

God's light continued shining
Sending him to Catholic U.
Then served in the UN where
He perceived a broader view

Always serving as a leader
With a servant's heart
A truly loving pastor
Who will always be a part

Of our family in New Hampshire
And always in our prayer
No matter where God sends him
To Rome or anywhere

In the light of a new mission
It may be difficult to see
God says to him "I'm leading you –
Come now, **Shine On** for me

"You are the light of the world. A city built on a hill cannot be hid. No one after lighting a lamp puts it under a bushel basket, but on the lampstand, and it gives light to all in the house. In the same way, let your light shine before others, so they may see your good works and give glory to your Father in heaven." Matthew 5:14-16

Rev. Msgr Anthony R. Frontiero
On the occasion of his assignment to study in Rome. April 2006

Friends (In Memory)

Remembering friends and praying for those
who have died is very important.

Often we remember to pray for our families
but may forget our friends and others who
may have been important in our lives
We may remember them in conversation
but neglect to pray for them.
I try to do both but I'm
sure there is room for improvement.

Here are a few verses of friends
I remembered in my poems.

Annette's Celebration

Today in celebration of
The life she lived on earth

Heaven joined the earthly choir
To sing the praises of her birth

She lived life with compassion
And love for God and family

She did her best to follow God
With true humility

She knew her Lord and Savior
And listened to his voice

Faithful to her call on earth
With God in every choice

Her life was filled with blessings
I'm sure she treasured every one

This was her special blessing
Mass celebrated by her son

Rev. Maurice Larochelle
Sainte Marie Parish - Pastor

Written after attending Annette Larochelle's funeral Mass
(the Mother of Father Maurice Larochelle) on January 2, 2004

Babsie's Roses

She came to spread among us
A precious rose bouquet
The fragrance of the Lord
Still lingers with us everyday

Her presence was anointed
Her prayers our Savior used
To bring healing and encouragement
And no one was refused

Her humor lightened burdens
 Her songs caused hearts to sing
And as she shared, she spoke
The Word of God in everything

Her stories we shall treasure
In the books she autographed
Remembering her joyfulness
Her smile and how she laughed

As she handed me the roses
That had been given her
 I received them with her blessing
And sensed God's Spirit stir

I kept them very carefully
Until each one dried out
In little baskets, reminiscent
Of what God's love is all about

The beauty of His boundless grace
This love beyond compare
Poured into every life to spread
His fragrance everywhere

Babsie Bleasdell
Conference at Sainte Marie ChurchManchester, NH
"The Holy Spirit, The Eternal Source of Every Gift"
Babsie Bleasdell, Speaker
November 13-15, 1998

"Thanks be to God who unfailingly leads us
on in Christ's triumphant train, and employs us
to diffuse the fragrance of his knowledge everywhere."
2 Corinthians 2:14

Esther McGowan – An Inspiration

Her way of showing kindness
Had a quality of its own

She did her job but most of what
She did remained unknown

She did things without fanfare
And truly loved to give

To those who were neglected
That's how she chose to live

She counseled troubled families
And truly loved each child

Her manner could be strong as steel
Yet loving, kind and mild

She dealt with those abused and
Scorned with true gentility

She care about the secret poor
And about their dignity

For those who knew her, she will
Be remembered for her love

Of helping those in need and
As she watches from above

She may still help some others
Who still may need to learn

There are always opportunities to
Give and look for no return

Esther McGowan died April 12, 1988.
Esther McGowan was a Senior Social Worker in the Child Welfare Division of Oneida County Dept. of Social Services, Utica, NY., until her retirement in 1987. For a time I had the privilege of being her supervisor in the Child Welfare Division. She was an inspiration to all her colleagues as well as her clients

Johnyne

Her life reflects the beauty
Of what the Lord has done
She shared the talents given her
Each and every one

Her love for all creation
Was reflected in her deeds
She magnified the Lord as
She relinquished her own needs

She cared for those around her
In her own quiet way
She moved with skill and patience
As a physician day by day

Devoted to her husband
And their children she loved much
And in caring for her patients
She brought God' healing touch

With her talent as an artist
And her creativity
She glorified the Lord
At home and in community

In her life, her faith sustained her
As God showed her the way
To enter into eternity
To hear the good Lord say

Well done, my faithful servant
You shared well the gifts on earth
Come now and share your Master's joy
The joy of your new birth

Johnyne Supulski Elechko, MD
11/22/1949 -12/06/2004

His master said to him.
"Well done, my good and faithful servant.
Since you were faithful in small matters,
I will give your greater responsibilities.
Come share your Master's joy".
Matthew 25:21

Justin – He's Special

This child you brought into the world
Now in eternity
Is in God's loving arms
And is rejoicing happily

The growing pains he felt have stopped
And now he is at peace
Just as God promised when you prayed
His love will never cease

The joy you felt when you first gazed
Upon his face at birth
Is what God felt when he arrived
In heaven from the earth

He is God's own creation
He loved him from the start
Just as He loves you too
And will begin to heal your heart

When God gives children to their
earthly parents, they don't know
How much time they'll be given here
To love and watch them grow

Each learns to trust in God, who says,
"The best is yet to be
I made him very special, be at peace
He's safe with me"

Written to his parents, Tom and Diane

Justin C. Cutler-
Age 17 years
Killed in auto accident
June 23, 1986

My Friend Gerry

A life well lived is a treasure
We each seek to present
To God a hundred-fold
For all the gifts to us He sent

This was my dear friend Gerry
Who loved all as Jesus taught
With all her heart and soul and
With her giftedness she wrought

Blessings beyond measure
For friends and family
Walking in the Word of God
That guided her to see

Her heart was always open
To help, to share, to pray
For anyone God sent to her
Or those along the way

Devoted wife and loving mother
She always put her family first
And for the Word of God
Insatiable was her thirst

Creative and unselfish
She carried out her daily tasks
Obedient to her Savior
In everything He asks

There were many who found Jesus
Because she showed the way
Or prayed for their healing or
Their loved ones gone astray

Her earthly journey ended
Yet she is with us still
We lovingly remember her
As we strive to do God's will

Gerry Deitz
My Friend & Prayer Partner
Photo – Medjugorje Pilgrimage 1988

Many are the women of proven worth but you have excelled them all. Proverbs 31:30

A True Sign of His Love

God grants the gift of children
And entrusts them to our care

Providing joy that comes through them
Though they are unaware

The purpose may be hidden
 As each life is lived out

And when they die we wonder
What this plan is all about

But God who is the giver of all
Good gifts knows that we

Who trust in Him are ready
To accept and let it be

For in the gift of children
We are given, there's a time

When we return the gift and say
"Not my will, Lord, but Thine"

When God sent your child to you
All the heavens sang above

A song of jubilation
To announce this gift of love

This life on earth was shortened
Perfection was achieved

Now she sings with the others
As in joy she is received

In the many days ahead
You'll realize somehow

That God loves us in ways that
Make no sense to us right now

Of all the gifts that come to us
From heaven up above

The precious gift of children is
A True Sign of His Love

Written to the parents of a 15 year old girl that I prayed for who died of Leukemia

Inspirational Verses

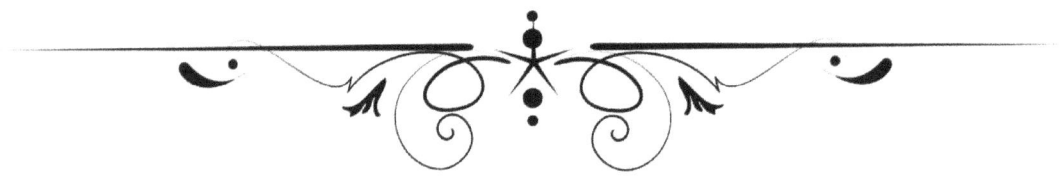

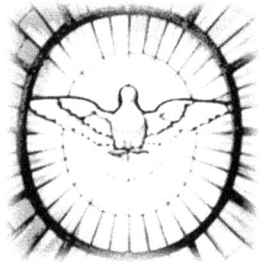

The inspiration for my verses is born
in prayer and quiet meditation. I like to sit with
the Lord and ask Him about many things.
My best conversations with Him often result in writing verses.
They cover a multitude of subjects in no particular order.

I believe the Holy Spirit reveals
"God's mind" on many things when we ask
and take the time to listen to what He has
to say to us.

For me and for many, I think that
poetry often expresses the inexpressible.

Loves Own Journey

Each heart began a journey
On that very special day

God breathed his love into each heart
In His sovereign way

He formed the fire of this love
To burn a loving flame

To share with one appointed
As He called each one by name

God's love is everlasting and
In this journey that's divine

Enjoy the wonder of this love
And every moment of this time

The Lord called me from birth,
from my mother's womb
he gave me my name.
Isaiah 49:1

Written for a newly engaged couple

His Inspiration

Like time
New thoughts are given
To bring about a change

Like Him
The greater works of God
Cause lives to rearrange

Like space
There are no limits
To what the Lord can do

Like Jesus Christ
Obedience is what
We're each called to

As high as the heavens are above the earth,
so high are my ways above your ways
and my thoughts above your thoughts.
Isaiah 55:9

Blessed Life Together

Together forever as
God's blessings unfold

May you bless each other
Even when you grow old

With a love that burns brightly
In your hearts today

May the joy of God's friendship
Enlighten your way

As you promise to be
A forever true friend

To each other, in His Love
Where there is no end

Where a lone man may be overcome,
two together can resist
A three-ply cord is not easily broken.
Ecclesiastes 4:12

Written for a young couple's wedding

His Treasures

From earth He formed these treasures
And breathed on each his breath

To bring to life a love to share
Together until death

Today these earthen vessels
Are awakened by his grace

To live this blessed union
Till you see Him face to face

...we hold these treasures in earthen vessels,
that surpassing power may be of God and
not from us. 2 Cor 4:7

Written for David and Donna Connare
Marriage Blessing
Feast of the Visitation 1995

Love Goes On

All creation longs to be one
With our Lord who made the earth

In this great universe in which
He chose to give each birth

The love that is eternal
Is the essence He supplies

As days pass by, each correlates
This love that never dies

Continuing to live this love
Trusting in His care

Creating rivers of expectation
Of love that's yet to share

With God and with each other
With an impetus that grows

In this river God creates to flow
It's destination, heaven knows

*All rivers go to the sea, yet never does the sea
become full. to the place where they go, they keep on
going. Ecclesiastes 1:7*

Written for anniversaries

First Anniversary

On this day one year ago
The heavens opened up

To pour new wine for you
To share this loving cup

God made this love so special
For it was meant to be

More special and more precious
With each anniversary!

*God looked at everything
He made and found it very good.
Genesis 1:31*

Changing Leaves

As I look up to praise the Lord
Who made the changing leaves

That dress once barren branches
With many colors on his trees

Each one is very different
Sometimes difficult to see

Yet on close inspection
One sees the unconformity

I think the green, the red, the gold
The orange and the brown

Are phases of new growth
To be lived as they fall down

As I perceive the changing leaves
I remember there's still spring

And all throughout the winter
God's nourishment will bring

A stronger tree with brand new leaves
That will be made to fall

God's leaves adorn his trees and then
His earth – that is their call!

God's Gifts

God's gifts ever available
To each and everyone

He sent the Holy Spirit
Through the gift of His own Son

He pours out gifts to use
To bless each in a special way

So enjoy this gracious bounty
Meant for each and everyday

The Spirit of the Lord shall rest upon him,
the spirit of wisdom and understanding,
the spirit of counsel and might,
the spirit of knowledge and
the fear of the Lord.
Isaiah 11:2

His Love Letter

God's Word
Is his love letter
Of outrageous love for you
He lived and died
For who you are
Not for what you do

He loves you
When you're happy
He loves you
When you're sad.
He loves you
Just the way you are
In the good times and the bad.

The Word made flesh
Among us,
Always living
Always true
Given freely
Never changing,
Is always there for you.

Jesus Christ is the same yesterday,
today and forever. Hebrews 13:8

Take Time

Take time
To share
God's word today

Take time
To hear
"I am the way"

Take time
To stop
To rest
To hear

"I'm with you always,
have no fear"

His Way

Live a life of kindness
In the love of God alone

Walk the path of Jesus Christ
Make His mercy known

Listen to The Word of God
And live this gift of love

Share His true compassion
Poured out from up above

Humble yourself daily
Before His holy throne

Pray for strength to walk His Way
Until He takes us home!

Show Me, Lord

Show me Lord, the way to go
Show me Lord, I want to know

Let me hear your word today
Help me know just what to say

Nothing that you ask of me
Will be too much for I am free

You've nurtured me in many ways
I could not have planned these days

Let me hear that perfect voice
Words of wisdom, God's own choice

Then I shall be free to choose
So my life you'll freely use

"My sheep hear my voice;
I know them, and they follow me."
John 10:27

Listen to God's Voice

When days are filled with clamor
And thoughts seem to collide
When other pressures plague you
And there is no place to hide

Stop for just a moment
- Listen to God's voice -

When your day is challenged
And your patience has grown thin
Even when you're feeling great
Whatever place you're in

Give yourself a breather
- Listen to God's voice -

When you have no answers
Even when you do
Remember the Holy Spirit
Is alive and well in you

Just accept His precious gift
- Listen to God's voice –

Therefore, as the Holy Spirit says
"Oh, that today you would hear
his voice". Hebrews 3:7

Written for my grandson, Daniel P. Dunn
Beginning college at Fairfield University, CT

Graduation

A new way is open
The road ahead is clear

Brand new beginnings
For a new way this year

New goals are waiting
For you to pursue

Dreams for a lifetime
Made just for you

If you "follow the Lamb"
In all that you do

He'll supply all your needs
And your dreams will come true

"Look, there is the Lamb of God
who takes away the sin of the world."
John 1:29

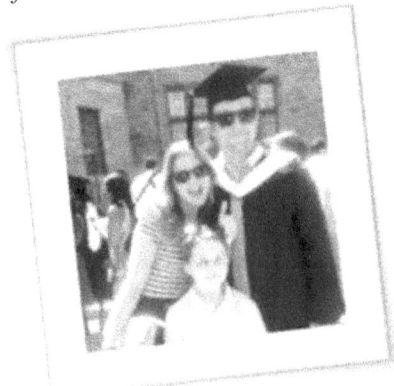

Dan's Fairfield Graduation
with Mari-Briege and Patrick Dunn

His Kind and Compassionate Way

Live a life of kindness
In the love of God alone

Walk the path of Jesus Christ
To make his mercy known

Listen to the Word of God
And live this gift of love

Share his true compassion
That's poured out from above

Humble yourself daily
Before his holy throne

Pray for strength to walk his way
And worship God alone

*Be kind to one another, compassionate,
forgiving one another as God has
forgiven you in Christ.
Ephesians 4:32*

His Consoling Heart

The pain of separation is so deep
It seems there is no cure

But from the heart of Jesus
There is power to endure

He gives love to sustain us
And reminds us - in His Name

We can go on, no matter what,
Because He's still the same

It's painful to lose loved ones,
Our grief remains as they depart

His love is everlasting
He consoles us from His heart

*Jesus Christ is the same
yesterday, today, and forever.
  Hebrews 13:8*

A Mother's Heart

A heart that listens
And always hears

A heart that nurtures
And calms all fears

A heart that's open
No matter the wrong

A heart filled with joy
Overflowing with song

A heart graced that prays
God will heal every pain

A heart that gives freely
Again and again!

*Mary treasured all these things
and reflected on them in her heart.
Luke 2:19*

His Fashion Statement

The fashions of true value
Worn by women everyday

Shine brightly with God's glory
A fashion statement of His way

Clothed in the holy garments
Of true praise and gratitude

Perfumed with God's fragrance
And a loving attitude

Fruits of the Holy Spirit
Evident from head to toe

Walking daily in His Spirit
To portray a holy glow

*Many are the women of proven worth
but you have excelled them all.
Proverbs 31:30*

*Written for Women of Mary,
Sainte Marie Parish*

Mary, God's Flower

In considering her motherhood
Reflect upon this thought

Mary's life was like a flower
One that can't be bought

Consider how she blossomed with
God's fragrance to pervade

The universe so all would know
The reason she was made

She bloomed and flowered in beauty
Amidst the pain and strife

As she allowed the Holy Spirit
To lead and fill her life

Every flower has a season in
God's timing for full bloom

Yet those who lack this fragrance
Still tell Jesus - "there's no room"

Called to be Christ-bearers
In God's Word to be well shod

Like Mary, with God's fragrance
May we always bloom for God!

They will bloom with abundant flowers
and rejoice with joyful song.
Isaiah 35:2a

Mary, Mother of His Love

Her arms extended to the world
Mary, Queen of Peace

Embraces all and prays that love
For God in each increase

She gave her heart completely
As she bore God's only Son

She stands in love and prays
His broken body will be one

Our hope for peace can only come
Through Jesus Christ, Our Lord

His Holy Mother Mary whose
Heart was pierced with evil's sword

Still ponders on these things and
Prays God's Spirit from above

Will fill each heart to praise Him
With the Mother of His Love

Mary treasured all these things and
pondered them in her heart.
Luke 2:19

Be Still in Him

Sounds of earth are silent power
Everywhere you are
Like sounds of heavenly blessings
Or a blinking star

Witness all the growth around you
All the growing things
Things of beauty and of color
And the joy each brings

As the leaves change quietly
To red and gold and brown
Not a sound will be heard
As they come tumbling down

As the grass keeps growing
There's not a single sound
Still it beautifies the earth
Covering the ground

Daily the sun will rise and set
It's beauty to observe
The creator of the colors
Is the God we serve

God provides his beauty
Always there to see
To remind our restless hearts
Rest in Him and let it be

God the master painter
Paints the canvas of our days
Reminding us be still and soon
We'll see His loving ways

Thoughts in Prayer

Songs of praise and worship
Help when we're depressed

As the music fills the air
In Him we take our rest

Angels join the chorus
And help keep the mind

Peaceful and receptive
To his love and soon we find

Cares and worries dissipate
In His abyss of love

And bubble up with a new joy
That comes from above

God the Father showers hope
And plants in us new seeds

In the Name of Jesus
Cares for all our needs

The Holy Spirit fills the spaces
And times when we felt lost

He removes the pain and sorrow
And absorbs the cost!

Be still and know that I am God…Is 46:11

Praise the Lord!

Sharing Losses

Sharing losses brings about
A calm way to be healed
When your heart is aching
It is painfully revealed

Senses are cued by your loss
Nothing seems the same
Even conversation's hard
When you hear the name

It triggers a reaction --
Perhaps you thought was healed
But God knows that we need to cry
And opens pain that's sealed

Just let the balm of Gilead
Pour over you today
And as the love of Jesus
Washes over you, He'll say

My child, I understand your pain
And I will show the way
As you look to me for help,
Your heart will mend -- so pray

For those who do not know me
Who still need to be free
So each may know I mourn their loss
If they will share with me

He Turned My Mourning Into Dancing

I grieved and grieved – and all my tears
Dried up and were no more

My heart so pierced, the crying ceased
No one could heal this sore

Then I heard the Lord whisper –
You are my own delight

He took me by the hand and said –
I'll give you holy sight

I pondered what He meant
And slowly I began to see

The way of truth and freedom –
To praise God and let it be

His love replaced my grieving
Each day a gift – a new surprise

Then my mourning turned to dancing –
His joy knows no compromise!

You changed my mourning into dancing.
You took off my sackcloth and clothed me with
gladness.
Psalm 30:11

A Tender Heart

Today in prayer, reflecting on
The sad day our dog died
I said-Lord, do you think it strange
I felt so sad I cried?

I asked Him if He ever had
A pet like a true friend
I wondered how he'd feel when
That companion met its end

He answered me in scripture-
That should a sparrow fall
It is written – Our Father –
Who is in heaven sees it all

He knows and counts each hair
That grows on every single head
He cares about your sad heart and
The dog you loved that's dead

He then reminded me that
Nothing living here on earth
Is meant to last forever
There is death as well as birth

He told me many loving things
About the time he gives
For fun and consolation with
His creatures while each lives

He also said that to each one
Who mourns a loss, He's near
He draws them closer to his heart
Where love casts out all fear

He said – I often use my animals
To bring both joy and fun
A caring time to be found
Of great value to each one

He then went on to say that
As the days go by
I'd be so grateful that
He gifted me to cry

Because the tender hearted
Are drawn close to God's own Son
The heart that is so tender has
Much to share with everyone

Duchess 2014
Jim and Meghan Vasil's Sheltie

He Hears

My heart cried out in pain but
There was no one to hear

I felt my world around me
Falling down and in my fear

I anguished and lamented
Was so distraught I cried

Then suddenly I thought of
Jesus Christ and how he died

I said, "Lord, why did you let
Those cruel men torture you?"

He said, "It's plain to see that
You've suffered torture too"

"I know, Lord, I replied, "but I'm
Not God, what can I do?

You are the King of glory and
You let them kill you too

He took my hand and sat me down
And said some simple things

Like – do you like flowers
Rainbows or a bird that sings

I told Him yes but that is not
What's really on my mind

He answered - be at peace
Keep things simple and you'll find

You need not worry - just believe
I'm always at your side

So you can have the best
Of all things and enjoy the ride

I have so much to give you
In this life and one day soon

You'll look back on this time and
Know today right in this room

The Lord of Lord, who is the Christ
Messiah, Morning Star

Wants you to know you're loved
He loves you just the way you are!

Written for a young woman who was struggling.

His Healing Word

His Word is everlasting
Bearing power to restore

To new life and to heal
He is with us forevermore

Divinity his nature
He reminds us He was man

He brings joy from human sorrow
Indeed we know He can

The Word made flesh still dwells
Among us every single day

Impressing us to lean upon Him
Joyfully and say

He is the Living Word sent forth
each day to rescue me

With thanks, declaring all His works
I will shout joyfully

He sent his word to heal them
and to snatch them from destruction.
Psalm 107:20

God Heals

Let the balm of Gilead
Pour over you today

As our God continues
His work in you, I pray

The bounty of his riches
Will enliven you

As fills you with His blessings
And heals your body too!

Heal me Lord, that I may be healed,
save me that I may be save,
for it is you whom I praise.
Jeremiah 17:14

Praise The Mighty Healer

Praise Jesus, Our Savior
Who parts the raging seas

Praise Him, who paid the price
For our suffering and disease

Praise God, who gives us daily bread
And teaches us to pray

Praise the Holy Spirit,
Who helps us day by day

As we praise the Mighty Healer,
On his Holy Word we stand

Together as God walks with us
To safety on dry land

He changed the sea to dry land;
through the river they passed on foot.
Therefore, let us rejoice in him,
who rules by might forever.
Psalm 66:6,7

His Healing Presence

Bring all your cares to Jesus
Bring him your anxious heart

His answer will be given
As gently he'll impart

The grace to know and love him
As he shares his healing balm

In His Presence, see him smile & say
I'm here - be still - be calm

He woke up, rebuked the wind,
and said to the sea, "Quiet! Be still".
The wind ceased and there was a great calm.
Mk. 4:39

Angels

I have a great devotion to the angels, especially to my guardian angel, Eva. Some may think this devotion is meant for children or feel they have outgrown the guardian angel prayer. It has always been a part of my prayer each day to pray to my guardian angel and it has become even more important to me as an adult.

In 1986, I began to pray more fervently about the angels. There seemed to be a new emphasis on the importance of angels in some prayer groups. There were more teachings on angels to dispel the various new age ideas about angels. Praying to our own guardian angel was encouraged and even referring to our angel by name.

One of the leaders of a prayer group I attended loaned me a teaching tape that was mainly scriptures about the angels. One day while driving home, I popped the tape into the tape deck and almost immediately I heard in my heart, "your angel's name is Eva". I shut the tape off to pray. I was astonished.

The name Eva was very unfamiliar to me. I have no friends or relatives with that name. As I prayed the Lord brought to mind a recent teaching about the true AVE of Mary; namely; to be available, vulnerable and expectant. I also recalled that Eva is Ave in reverse. Eve was the disobedient woman in the beginning described in the Old Testament. Mary, the obedient woman described in the New Testament, turned everything around for all of humanity. It was so simple. It made sense.

As soon as I arrived home that day, I called my spiritual director. I shared all this with him. He shared my belief in what I heard and thought. After our conversation, I felt affirmed. So I began to pray to my guardian angel by name, Eva.

Three years later, when I relocated from Utica, NY to Manchester, NH, I had been praying to my guardian angel over all the details of relocating including helping me locate a parish. I felt the nudge to go to Sainte Marie Church which is on the West side even though my children were attending a parish on the East side. I went to confession at Sainte Marie on Saturday. On Sunday we attended Mass there. While sitting in a pew in the center aisle, I looked up to the right of the altar and was struck by the most beautiful stained glass window depicting the Annunciation. There written on the window as plain as can be were the words EVA on the left side and AVE on the right side. I immediately knew this was a sign for me. I have never seen this written on any window in any other church even to this day.

After Mass, I told my children I was joining the parish. "Are you sure" They asked, "you've only lived here two weeks?" My answer was simply, "Jesus is here, The Holy Spirit is here, the Mother of God is here, and so is my guardian angel, Eva. Her name is right on the window with the blessed Mother. I'm staying. This is where I belong".

On the following Monday, I called and joined the parish and made an appointment for spiritual direction with the priest that had heard my confession. That was September 1989.

My Favorite Window in Sainte Marie Church

Baby's Angel

A new life created
God's own design

An angel appointed
This moment in time

For now and forever
Stands ready to keep

Sweet baby protected
Awake or asleep

Your Guardian Angel

On the day you were created
God appointed especially

Your own guardian angel
One you cannot see

May this be a reminder
Of God's protection everyday

You have a guardian angel
To keep you from harm's way

For to his angels he has given command about you,
that they guard you in all your ways. Psalm 91:11

Holy Angels

May the holy angels
Everyday

Lift and lighten
Up your way

I pray the angels
Gather round

As you stand firm
On holy ground

The angel of the Lord
encamps around those
who fear him and
delivers them.
Psalm 34:8

Angels of New Life

Let the light of Jesus Christ
Ablaze now in your heart

Shine brightly in your life anew
Enjoying this new star

As you walk with confidence
In Him who is the way

God provides his angels
to be with you come what may

Then the Lord said to them, "Take off
the sandals from your feet, for the place
where you are standing is holy ground."
Acts 7:33

Christmas Angels

Everywhere in every place
the Lord sends to earth

His angels to protect us
and proclaim his holy birth

He sent Gabriel to Mary
with a message to impart

To prepare for Jesus' coming
as He grew within her heart

The Lord has many angels
each with a job to do

For every Christmas season
there are Christmas angels too

So be aware of angels that
help us on our way

For myriads of angels are
dispatched for Christmas Day!

And suddenly there was with the angel
a multitude of the heavenly host,
praising God and saying, "Glory to
God in the highest heaven, and on earth
peace among those whom he favors!"
Luke 2: 13, 14

Healing Angels

God's healing power is
Poured out everywhere

Through many holy servants
Who are often unaware

He sends his holy messengers
To help us and proclaim

The power of His healing
Is done In Jesus' Name

Peter said, "I have neither silver nor gold,
but what I do have I give you:
in the name of Jesus Christ,
the Nazorean, rise and walk."
Acts 3:6

Traveling Angels

As you set out on a journey
Regardless of the time or day

God will send his holy angel
To accompany you on the way

Your way will be protected
Angelic company you'll keep

His protection will surround you
Until your journey is complete

… a good angel will go with him
and his journey will be successful,
and he will return you unharmed.
Tobit 5:22

Angels of Encouragement

Look all around you
And decide to believe

God sends out his angels
For you to receive

That comforting whisper
You think you can hear

Believe God is with you
Be at peace, have no fear

For to his angels, he has given
command about you, that they
guard you in all your ways.
Psalm 91:11

More Memories

Many occasions gave me opportunities to write verses for my family. I wrote and made birthday cards, thank you cards, anniversary cards, cards for every occasion. I always tried to convey some meaningful and loving message. I think they all enjoyed them and it was fun for me, especially writing for my grandchildren.

Baking for the holidays has always been an important part of the festivities, especially for Christmas. As you can imagine, I was trying to groom all of my daughters to take over the baking one day. As the years passed, they all became very proficient in this great art of baking. Many recipes became tradition. Phone calls for lost or misplaced recipes were endless, no matter how many times I shared them. So I found a solution in a Christmas gift I made for each one of my daughters.

For their Christmas gifts in 2005, I decided to put together a recipe book with some of the favorite recipes in it which is featured on the following page.

A Recipe Solution

What happened to that recipe
I thought it was right here

It's a must-make for Christmas
We have it every year

Why is it I can't find it now
I make it all the time

It may be in "that special place"
Of no order or design

Or did it get dripped on
And set aside so I'd rewrite

Put right where I would find it
But now gone out of sight

Woe is me if I don't find it
Then however will I cook

Here's your recipe solution
Just put them in this book

This recipe keeper was my Christmas gift to each one of my daughters in 2005 complete with some of our favorite recipes

The Moore Girls
Meghan (top)
Kelly, Teresa, Kimberly

Unforgettable Years

In the year 2005, my alma mater,
St. Elizabeth College of Nursing honored
the Class of 1955 at the annual alumni
banquet on the occasion of our 50th
anniversary.

Sadly, I was unable to attend but I wrote
the following two verses to share.
These were some thoughts from those
truly unforgettable years. As I often have
said, "those were some of those good ole days
when we prayed for better times"!

One of my classmates, Marilyn Tyo, read these
poems at the banquet and shared with me that
they were the highlight of the evening.

Blessed Training in Reverence

Daily we learned reverence
Encountering Our Lord

At Mass, at prayer, in chapel,
In the patients on each ward

Respect for human life
True compassion for the sick

For suffering comes to everyone
A journey none would pick

Beyond science, skill & knowledge
We learned nothing is held bound

For in receiving Eucharist
Peace and healing may be found

Each day, at the break of dawn
As nurses we prepared

Each patient to receive Him
And with great reverence shared

A bell announced His Presence
A nun led with a holy light

Calling everyone to genuflect
Till they were out of sight

A nurse knelt at the entrance
Of every single ward

As each patient waited
To receive Our Lord

I remember now with gratitude
The joy that made my day

When at the last ward I knelt
And in a whisper, say

"Me too", Father,
Pointing to my heart

This gratitude for Eucharist
Still makes my day start

My devotion second nature
No need to rehearse

True reverence I practiced daily
As I became a Catholic Nurse

Sarah Jane Lavery
Student Nurse

Remembering 1955

Remember the "good ole days"
When we prayed for better times

We had some good ideas
That were not all "God's design"

We lived this special time of life
We were anxious to complete

And now in retrospect we see
Those struggling years were sweet

Who now knows what a "pinkie" is
Or wears a pocket watch

Do they still make hair nets
And rise for prayer at 6 o'clock

Who remembers how to "pull a cap"?
And the joy of "capping day"

We finally could wear our whites
And throw the pinks away

We cleaned our shoes with ether
When we were in a pinch

A neat appearance was expected
No one would give an inch

If we taped our stockings up
It hadn't better show

And if we didn't wear a girdle
Sister certainly would know

Sleeping in our underwear
When we were "on call"

Running through the tunnel
We gave it our all

Our dining hall was in the basement
But we would always hear

Maxine shout, "the door is open
The meal cart is here"

Remember diet kitchen
With each small mistake

The salt that ruined the custard
Barb did the whole blame take

How about Betty's salads
Sister was quick to lament

"Her salads were not smiling"
Who knew what that even meant

How about those days in surgery
What was high dusting for?

Hester and I remember
The "yucky" laundry chore

Night duty fostered humor
And little jokes we'd make

"Old time Nurse" a few of us
Would play to stay awake

Things that make us laugh now
Seem ridiculous at best

But that was what sustained us
And helped us with the rest

"Faithful to duty to the end, a good sport and a loyal friend"

Aurora Yearbook 1955
St. Elizabeth College of Nursing, Utica, NY

Thank You Holy Spirit

Over thirty five years ago, The Holy Spirit opened up my entire life to God in a way that I didn't know existed. I learned that Jesus still heals today as He did when He walked the earth and I experienced it more than once. I discovered that God had spiritual gifts for everyone to enjoy, including me.

I was raised Catholic and always tried to be faithful. Daily Mass, novenas and praying the rosary have always been a part of my life. However, through my involvement in the Catholic Charismatic Renewal, my whole life woke up to a personal relationship with Jesus Christ and to the power of the Holy Spirit. I experienced the Baptism in the Holy Spirit through a Life in the Spirit Seminar. I learned that although I received the Holy Spirit in Baptism, through the Sacraments and my Confirmation, there were gifts of the Holy Spirit yet to be released in my life. The gifts of praying in tongues and spontaneous prayer, praise and worship and prophecy and prayer for healing began to manifest in my spiritual life. The scriptures came alive for me and my personal prayer time increased. Everything was new.

Sometimes I would wake up in the middle of the night praising the Lord. One night I woke up in the middle of the night, wrote a verse and went back to sleep. In the morning, I read it. It was in perfect rhyme and there was a spiritual message contained in it. That was the first time I ever wrote a poem. I tried unsuccessfully to ask advice about this. So I got up earlier every morning to spend time with the Lord and He gave me a verse and understanding of it each day. That was in 1979 and I have written nearly every day since.

I share this because I never wrote a poem before I was baptized in the Holy Spirit. I had no desire to write poetry at all. I was an excellent student in English in school and liked to write. I was asked in later years why I did not pursue this kind of study. My answer is simple. "When you are the first of nine children to pursue higher education and your parents are not encouraging this, you do not announce that you are going to become a writer; you pick something that will earn you a living." So I became a nurse, like my aunt and namesake, Sarah Jane Lavery Madigan. Later on, when I became a Social Worker, I was often complimented on my narratives in keeping my records. I never gave that a second thought

 I believe the Holy Spirit ignites every good gift we have and gifts that lie dormant come alive. Writing has been a joy as well as a consolation to me over the years.
Thank you Holy Spirit!

Statue of Our Blessed Mother Mary
in St. Charles Children's Home Chapel, Rochester NH
Photo taken by Sister Mary Rose, DMML